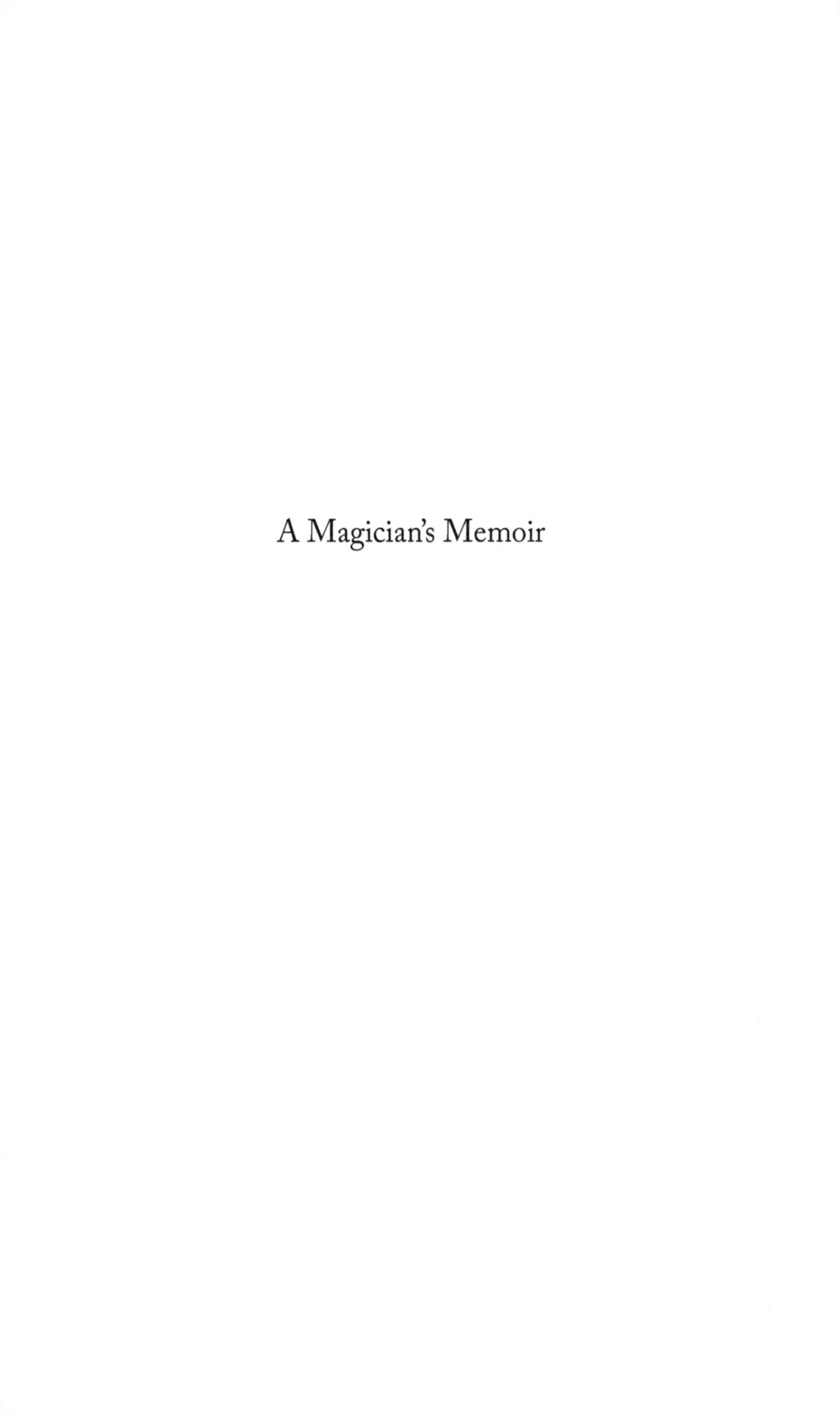

A Magician's Memoir

Jack Cain's A Magician's Memoir is an embodied perception of our unseen reality. It opens our eyes in this dark time to the human situation and its sacred roots. Through his extended encounters across the globe, Cain offers us the choice of affirming life, life with its unbreakable connection to the planet. A necessary read!

– David Appelbaum

A Magician's Memoir

The Pull of Spirit

Jack Cain

Epigraph Books
Rhinebeck, New York

First Edition

Paperback ISBN 978-1-960090-50-8
eBook ISBN 978-1-960090-51-5

Library of Congress Control Number 2023924199

Design and Layout: Jeffrey Macklin, Jackson Creek Press

Front cover: Aegean Sea walkway at the town of Çeşme near Izmir, Turkey.
Back cover: Brockville, Ontario, Canada looking across the St. Lawrence River at the hamlet of Morristown, New York.

Epigraph Books
22 East Market Street, Suite 304
Rhinebeck, New York 12572
(845) 876-4861
epigraphps.com

I dedicate this book to the angel of mercy
whose touch years ago ensured I would survive
to write what appears in the pages that follow.

Doorway to the Invisible, Framed
With Stepping Stone
Found near the great pyramid in Cholula, Mexico

The invisible world is constantly accessible and present around us wherever we are. It is not in some distant place to be discovered. The door that gives access to it is in us – it has never been anywhere else.

– Stéphane Allix, *When I Was Someone Else,*
Inner Traditions, 2021, p. 14.

1. The Fall of the Priestess

The Bolivian archeological site of Tiahuanaco is one of those ruins that seems to have been plundered constantly from the time it was abandoned. Even much of the restoration work is of doubtful authenticity since so little is known about the original civilization.

The Gate of the Sun, looking more like a doorway than a gate, presumably cracked in an earthquake and partially fallen down, has been set upright. When I look at the photograph of this gate in the Wikipedia article, I sense an almost imperceptible stirring – as if I am being invited to step through.

I hesitate a moment, then I do.

Trumpets and drums. A procession moves forward with stately grace. Held aloft is an image of the sun – intricate gold, blazing with the light of a clear sky day. Some are walking, some, in richly colored attire with ornaments of gold, are carried on palanquins.

A priestess dressed in red walks in front, chanting in the sacred language she has been taught since childhood.

> Vibrations
> Of the human voice
> Stirring the gods to life.
>
> Action in the visible world
> To engender a communication
> With the world unseen.

The procession reaches a pinnacle – the holy of holies. Each person has an appointed place. From the drumming and the regulated walking, the priestess now has entered the special state required for her to be a voice for the gods – so that action from the invisible world can appear in the visible world. All this is known and is very clearly understood.

The priestess knows that there are dangers. Has her purification been sufficiently deep? Have guides and allies come? What are the opposing forces? Can they be overcome so that her receptivity is finely honed? So that she can speak messages of only holy import.

Of gods and men
Where does the allegiance lie?
Forces. Forces tug.

She voices something she has not heard. Something she thinks ought to be said. Because what she heard made no sense to her. "Say it anyway," she was told. But she remains silent.

Clouds gather. Dark clouds that cover the sun.

Too late she realizes her mistake. She has fallen from grace. Silently, the gods mourn her fall.

The glory of the empire fades. Oblivion is inexorably now at hand.

The fall of the priestess.
Such is our fate.
We lose our way.

§§§

2. The Invisible World
Who Goes There?

"I readily believe that there are more invisible than visible Natures in the universe. But who will explain for us the family of all these beings, and the ranks and relations and distinguishing features and functions of each? What do they do? What places do they inhabit? The human mind has always thought the knowledge of these things, but never attended. Meanwhile I do not deny that it is helpful sometimes to contemplate in the mind, as on a tablet, the image of a greater and better world, lest the intellect, habituated to the petty things of daily life, narrow itself and sink wholly into trivial thoughts. But at the same time we must be watchful for the truth and keep a sense of proportion, so that we may distinguish the certain from the uncertain, day from night."

This quotation was adapted by the English poet Samuel Taylor Coleridge from Thomas Burnet, Archaeologiae philosophicae *(1692) p. 68 and placed as a Latin epigraph to the 1817 edition of his long poem "The Rime of the Ancient Mariner."*

The inquiry being recommended here is a nice outline of the exploration that led to *A Magician's Memoir: The Pull of Spirit*. The need for such an endeavor was reinforced for me many years ago by a quotation attributed to Saint John of the Cross painted on the wall of the food court in Montreal's busy central train station: "*Il faut aller des choses qu'on voit et qui n'existe pas aux choses qu'on ne voit pas et qui existe.*" ("We must move on from things which we see but which do not exist to things which we do not see but which do exist.")

As we embark on the ship of life, how are we to "distinguish the certain from the uncertain" with as much clarity as distinguishing day from night? How to distinguish the stirring of life from simple activity? Life is not the movement of the mechanism of a clock nor is it the running of a piece of computer software.

Crocuses push through the snow in spring. Lilies of the valley release their perfume. Such movement touches a sensitive and subtle part of us – if we're not dead. As the poet T.S. Eliot comments, watching throngs of people crossing London Bridge, "I did not know death had undone so many."

Crocuses

§

Dead Man's Gulch

Having just arrived in Mexico City, I am walking back to my cozy airbnb with bags of groceries from the supermercado. To accomplish this feat, I must cross the intersection of Avenida Revolución and another major artery: Barranca del Muerto. (Translation: Dead Man's Gulch – in the early 1900s it was a ravine used as a cemetery for unmarked graves. Today it's filled in and paved over.) Both of these multilane thoroughfares are packed with pedestrians, bicycles, cars, scooters, buses, and trucks. The subway station named Barranca del Muerto, whose symbol is two vultures, is nearby – the last stop southbound on the major north-south line, line 7, and a terminus for many suburban bus routes. As I'm walking, I am aware, having visited the city a number of times already, that, first of all, the traffic lights are what might be called "suggestions," and secondly, that who goes first is negotiated through eye contact with the driver who is about to run you down. Sometimes, adding a colorful flare to the mix, there are jugglers perched on the medians, performing their tricks. The whole scene is noisy, dirty, ugly, and appears to be totally chaotic.

As I walk on with my groceries and approach the intersection, I begin to cry. The wave of emotion overpowers all thought. I stop for a moment, stepping aside from the flow on the sidewalk. My body, my feet, all my senses tell me: "You are home." And in my heart I understand that I am weeping tears of happiness and relief. Once back in my lodgings, I pour myself a glass of red wine from the little bottle that my host has kindly left for me as a welcoming gift, and I raise my glass in a toast to the life that overcomes death.

§

A Boat

The image of a boat
Arises in my mind.
A simple wooden boat that is empty
But moving gently on calm water –
Not drifting but following some invisible path.
And then I notice
What I did not see at first
That there is, in the center of the boat,

Resting on its wooden floor
A treasure chest.
And I hear the words,
"Steer carefully now
So that your treasure is secure."
Steer?
I wonder at this word.
Is it I who steers this boat?

"Yes, it is you who steers.
Awaken now to what you carry within you
And to the direction
That you have been given to follow."

"But I know nothing of all this –
Neither the boat nor the treasure."

"You speak too fast.
Long have you known
And you know it still.
Awaken now
And live all of what you are.
The water is deep
And the path is long
But you have help you cannot see.
Trust.
Breathe.
And all will be well.

§§§

3. Fulfilling Who I Am
Entry Point

I am standing with my arms raised and my head tilted back. A shaft of blue light that is not light descends, passing through me into the Earth. A deep, intense, vibrant blue. A sacred function is being fulfilled. I submit to its action as I have been directed to do. I am male.

I am in a pyramid. My body is a ceremonial object, engaged in a transmission for the life of the planet on which this pyramid rests.

As I write these lines, the planet is suffering today in a way it was not millennia ago, because what I was doing in that distant age is no longer regularly being done now. As I enter into these perceptions, I am stretched across two periods of time – Egypt then and the current boreal wildness now. But there is only one time, there is only now, what is happening now.

The blue light acts in both directions – down and back up. It is a communication, a communion. There is no thinking, no mental activity. There is only feeling, a deep feeling of the sanctity of what I have been chosen to fulfill.

My skin is light brown. There are gold ornaments and I am dressed in white linen. I have sandals on my feet. I feel very alone. Alone without human company. But this feeling is irrelevant to the function being performed.

My life is devoted to the world of spirit and to bringing a connection to that world.

I hear the name Amon-Ra. I embody Amon-Ra. This name resounds within me.

§

How could I have fallen so far away from this?

The understanding was so clear then; so distant now. There was a word for that light then; there is no word for it now. To bring these two times together is terrifyingly unbelievable. There is no doubt about the reality of the light I am seeing. I am in it. But it is in the past. I am asked, "What do you need to bring it into the now?"

I just did. Or... that is what just took place.

But it is a connection that overwhelms my emotions.

The connection ought not to be with my emotions.

Why am I crying?

Idiotic.

Who I am becomes who I was; who I was becomes who I am.

There is no room for a betrayal of self any more.

§

The Next Step

Trylus[1]: From this insight, from this vision, what is my next step? What is my direction to be?

Guide: *Remain in the light and transmit.*

Trylus: Must the gods of Egypt be re-invoked?

Guide: *No. Certainly not. They belong to another time and another world. But what they represent must come to be experienced and known, as you have recently done, a little, in listening to what the eagles were telling you.*

Trylus: How can what was known then become known now?

Guide: *Focus. Use your physical body as you just did to return to the transmission of blue light.*

Trylus: I am hungry for knowledge from that time.

Guide: *Do not hunger for knowledge. Hunger for experience.*

Trylus: I experience witnessing the rising of Sirius. It is an ache in my belly.

Guide: *Allow your belly to speak to you. Feel the shift in your foundation. Feel the change in your orientation. Feel.*

Trylus: The familiar world crumbles, topples. Destruction. Chaos. Screaming masses.

Guide: *Sirius is rising. Fear not. You are not alone and you are protected. The beam of blue light is still accessible. Be vigilant in your merging with its light.*

§

What the Eagles Said

The space between
Between planets in one or another star system
The arc of that, the arch of that,
the canopy of that
Moving down, down, and down
Down into a movement in the chest
Infinitely fine
Slight vertigo when faced with this immensity
Listen, listen, listen hard and fast
We speak to you
We are between
Between the branches
Between the interstices of thought

Between the blue threads of time
We speak to you because you are needed
You all are needed
We all are needed
We are
And in our are-ness there is a flow
Reach out
Reach out and touch this flow
Feel its texture
Taste, savor its elemental nature
Be in this larger world
The choice is yours
We await you
This current awaits you
Consciousness awaits you
Be

Eagles

§§§

4. Blue Alchemy
Mist

As we begin our tour of the cathedral in the town of Chartres, a two-hour train ride southwest from Paris, the tour guide tells us how lucky we are to be visiting the cathedral on a cold, rainy, misty day. She explains that such weather shows off most dramatically the blue in the cathedral's stained-glass windows – windows that have survived intact from the 13th century. No one today knows how that intense color was produced – it is said that the formula has been lost. Most visitors agree that the color is mysteriously poignant.

Chartres Cathedral, Photo: Chantale Riopel

The mystery deepened for me when I took on the translation from French to English of Geneviève Dubois's *Fulcanelli dévoilé* (*Fulcanelli Revealed*). In 1926, a book titled *Le Mystère des cathédrales* appeared under the authorship of Fulcanelli – clearly a pseudonym. The book became famous and engendered a renewal of interest in alchemy but Fulcanelli's identity remained unsolved until Dubois undertook her detailed research. My English translation appeared as: *Fulcanelli and the Alchemical Revival: The Man behind the Mystery of the Cathedrals*, Rochester, Vermont, Destiny Books, 2006.

Relevant here is not the authorship, which was complex, but the fact that two men involved in the Fulcanelli book, René Schwaller de Lubicz and Jean-Julien Champagne, collaborated, using alchemy, to successfully reproduce the substances that must have been used for both the blue and the red in the Chartres windows. On page 88 we read: "He (René Schwaller) described for me (André VandenBroeck, author of *Al-Kemi, a Memoir*, p. 190) the separation of sulfur carried out on copper. A colored luminosity spread over the cinders of the material. The tinting mass represented the essential dyeing within the colored glass."

Dubois summarizes this process as follows:

"The Chartres glass is dyed in its mass by the volatile spirit of metals."

It seems this knowledge, this alchemical secret, has now been lost again.

The transmutation of metals
My heart listens
Intently.

That particular blue
What does it touch?
What part?

I am pulled
Pulled up
By the blue.

The Rose Window of Chartres Cathedral,
Photo: Chantale Riopel

§

Talking to Blue

Trylus: In returning to the sensation in the body as blue from the Chartres windows enters me, I feel a subtle movement begin in my chest. Tell me blue, what is this?

Blue: *Just follow the movement. What happens?*

Trylus: I begin to breathe more deeply. And there is a subtle hiving at the nape of the neck.

Blue: *And?*

Trylus: Suddenly, you are standing before me. Smiling. What does this mean?

Blue: *It means we have work to do together.*

Trylus: What work is that?

Blue: *Together, we must send the enlivening vibration of this color into the swirling ocean of humanity.*

Trylus: We?

Blue: *Yes. I provide the intelligence and you provide your incarnated body. It is essential to have both.*

Trylus: That is hard for me to understand.

Blue: *Don't try to understand. Return to following your breathing and the movement of the color blue within your body.*

Trylus: I am breathing the sun and the moon and the planets. And I am fed by that.

Blue: *And as that food converts to energy within you, I direct its movement out into that swirling ocean where it will activate certain elements for a universal good.*

Trylus: Incredible.

Blue: *Not incredible. Lawful.*

Trylus: It's beyond me.

Blue: *No. You are beyond it.*

Trylus: I repose in a smile.

Blue: *As do I.*

§§§

5. Mr. Dark
Teotihuacan

My friend Michel insists that, given the very limited duration of my first visit to Mexico in 2013, I absolutely must visit Teotihuacan on the eastern outskirts of the city. We begin the two-hour drive from central Mexico City right away.

No one knows who built, perhaps some two thousand years ago, this pyramid site and the extensive city that once surrounded it. There is speculation that its name, which is not likely its original name but one given by later civilizations that overran it, means "The place were men become gods."

Traveling
Gives the illusion
Of going somewhere.

And yet, on this trip, there *is* a deeper sense of going somewhere. It is Easter Sunday, March 31st 2013, and the pyramid site is packed with visitors. Foreigners like myself are rare. We join a very long line of those wanting to climb to the top of the main pyramid. The line snakes around two sides of the enormous structure. Suddenly, I have an odd perception, a feeling or visual insight, and I say to Michel, "You know, the most important part of this structure is below ground." "Interesting you should say that, Jack," Michel replies. "There is a special room under the pyramid which is not open to the public. When the Dalai Lama visited Mexico, he was given permission to meditate there."

Stone
Laid on stone
For a purpose.

Teotihuacan: Looking down from part way up

After climbing the main pyramid, we split up and Michel drives his car to the other side of the enormous compound so it would be there close by when we had traversed the site and were ready to leave. This allows me to walk on my own between the Pyramid of the Sun we had just climbed, along the long, wide processional way toward the smaller Pyramid of the Moon. As I walk, the rhythm of my breathing changes – it is suddenly slow and deep. The spatial perception of the processional way wavers as if it might disappear. If I could have been alone on the site something more might have taken place, but, in fact, although this altered perception lasts five or ten minutes, nothing further happens. And yet, and yet… as I write this now, eight years later, in 2021, I am back there once again, feeling the special state and totally certain that a huge experience is just out of reach. It is in me, but I cannot access it. As I maintain my focus, something begins to form. It feels too strong. There is fear. Better not. Better not. At least, not now.

Awareness
Wavers
What does it mean to see?

§

Having Words with Mr. Dark

Later in my 2021 writing process, the following occurs:

Today I keep being distracted and don't apply myself to my writing. Consequently, I stub my toe badly. It feels like it's broken.

As I reconnect to the altered reality I had experienced when walking alone from the "Pyramid of the Sun" to the "Pyramid of the Moon" – which were originally called simply "My Father" and "My Mother" – I see a dark figure, clearly male, but I can make out no features and it is more like a silhouette.

And I receive an indication: "Here is why you fear authority – it has little to do with events in your current life."

I ask my angel to accompany me as I address this dark figure.

Trylus: I feel that you want to crush me like a bug.

Mr. Dark: That is accurate. And I have good reason for the force I emit.

Trylus: Tell me why.

Mr. Dark: You betrayed me.

Trylus: You mean when I turned my back on the dark and dedicated myself to the light – for ever.

As those words ring within me, wind brings down a tree on our house and the room I'm working in. A shock, but it turns out the damage is minimal.

Mr. Dark: We had a pact and you broke it. There are no words that can express my anger and disgust.

Trylus: Here in what now is called Teotihuacan there used to be both dark sorcerers and light sorcerers. My angel says that you and I must stand side by side. Now.

Mr. Dark: I curse your angel.

Trylus: And yes, well you might. But you also know your curse cannot touch the angel. And you know that there are forces incommensurably greater than those commanded by either you or me. Greater even than those of my angel.

Mr. Dark: I know that. But I will struggle against them just the same. That is my fate.

Trylus: The calendar turns. I am speaking to you from the emerging fifth world that is just beginning.

Mr. Dark: I know.

Trylus: Embrace me.

Mr. Dark: Why?

Trylus: Through this embrace a ruby will form. It will provide guidance to the fifth world – guidance in balancing light and dark. You will be rewarded.

Mr. Dark: You are tricking me.

Trylus: It is the powers that be who are urging this embrace not I. This can be your destiny. And you can struggle still if you find that is what you need to do.

Embrace me.

And thus a ruby forms.

§§§

6. The Call of Crystalline Limestone

May 12, 1954: Three mining prospectors sit down to rest and eat their lunch on a gently sloping outcrop of crystalline limestone, a type of rock sometimes called white marble. This limestone is a much softer sedimentary rock compared to the very hard granite that makes up most of the Canadian Shield. The Shield is the ancient core of the North American continent. Most of it lies deeply buried, but parts are visible in Ontario having been exposed by glaciation. The limestone was formed under high pressure over great periods of time.

Gradually these men become aware that the outcrop they are sitting on is densely covered in carved images. The petroglyphs are hard to make out at first because both the carved impression and the surface are white. Feeling the rock with their fingers is more revelatory than looking.

This is how what are now called "The Peterborough Petroglyphs" were discovered in an isolated, wooded area three miles (five km) from Stony Lake, 30 miles (50 km) from the nearest big town of Peterborough, and 150 miles (240 km) northeast of Toronto.

Later, in order to photograph them, the carved impressions were filled with charcoal.[2]

The force
Of the crystalline limestone
Calls.

Calls
To the shaman's skill:
And to his soul.

Tell and recount
Recount and show
The upper and lower worlds.

Our middle world
Hungers
For what he has found there.

Our souls face starvation
And the Earth trembles
Beneath our feet.

Petroglyph image 1:
Figure walking forward.
Its head is a radiant sun

Here is the way:
The way forward
Into becoming.

Left leg behind right,
Knees bent,
Body inclined.

Circling the neck
Circling, circling
Until thinking becomes a sun and shines.

Oh, so far
So far above the body
Sun within sun

Twelve harmonic rays
Announce arrival
At the I within the I.

> Petroglyph image 2:
> A boat with passengers, rocking.
> Masts of sun and moon. And a
> rudder beyond treachery.

Riding the wave
Accompanied
By brother sun and sister moon.

> Petroglyph image 3:
>
> A shaman figure with rattle and lasso.
> The top half of his head is excised,
> And replaced by a tall symbolic triangle.

The shaman's head
Must be transmuted
To abstract form.

The rattle in his hand
Draws a galactic lasso:
And I ride my eagle.

Together,
Homeward
We fly.

§§§

7. An Inuit Drummer

In darkness
An Inuit man is drumming the starry universe
Into existence.
Stepping on stardust,
His stride is strong and vigorous
As he moves to the other side of night.

Pulling him forward
His drum is a circle
A circle of sound
That ripples out through time and space
Reaching through the stars to a promise
That quivers in his song.

Sing now sing
Oh sing your holy song
For all the suffering souls
Whom you are showering here.

Emerging from warm darkness and from stone,
Our universe resonates
Exquisitely
In spirit
Within us
Within us each and every one.

An Inuit Drummer
Carver: ᐊᐃᓯᐊᓯ ᑯᐸᓕ (Iziasie Kopalie), Iqaluit
Iqaluit Fine Art Studios, +1 867 979-5578

§§§

8. Jupiter
The Probe

On April 27, 1973, in the Radio Physics Laboratory at the Stanford Research Institute, Menlo Park, California, an experiment called the "Jupiter Probe" was conducted. The probe was proposed and carried out by the intrepid Ingo Swann (1933-2013) who, leaving his body safely in California, projected his consciousness to the planet of miracles, Jupiter. He made his report to two other participants in the project: Russell Targ and Harold Sherman. I will summarize here what he had to say.

He first mentioned that the planet had stripes and he surmised that it had a huge hydrogen mantel 80,000 to 120,000 miles above its surface. He saw glittering crystals in its atmosphere and then realized what he called "stripes" were bands of crystals like the rings of Saturn but much closer to the planet and within its atmosphere. As he descends into Jupiter's atmosphere, he says, "It feels good here." (Maybe the tradition that those born under Jupiter are jovial is not so far-fetched!) He ends his report by saying that the crystal layers look beautiful from the outside but from the inside they look like eerie gas clouds of yellow light and rainbows.[3]

In 1973, the year of this probe experiment, Jupiter's rings were as yet unknown to science. In 1979, the Voyager I spacecraft photographed the rings, which NASA then categorized as "Main Ring," "Halo," and "Gossamer Rings."

§

On Friendship

Trylus: Mr. Swann, given the success of this exploration, you must have subsequently made other voyages, right?

Swann: *Of course.*

Trylus: I was interested in your comment about feeling good. It seems related to Edgar Cayce's critique of astrology – that the influence of the planets on one's life is not nearly as powerful as the amount of time one actually spends *on* a given planet.

Swann: *Cayce's sources are sound and reliable. The comforting expansiveness I felt being near Jupiter continues to be a support for me.*

Trylus: Now that you have left your twentieth century earthly body behind permanently, do you still travel to locations in the universe?

Swann: *Yes, I do, but that is determined by my relationships.*

Trylus: Relationships? Can you say more?

Swann: *Just as in the life I have left, so now too I travel based on the needs that arise in my working relationships with each individual – human or non-human, incarnate or discarnate.*

Trylus: Is such travel easier now?

Swann: *Actually, "travel" is not even an appropriate word; travel is not necessary because of the non-local nature of reality. I target a destination and I am there. Just as it was with the Jupiter probe, now too, being here with you, a fellow writer and traveler, there is no time or space to traverse. I am here instantly with no gap.*

Trylus: When you say "working" can you elaborate on the work you are doing?

Swann: *It is not that different from my work in the incarnation I left in 2013. Gurdjieff put it rather well: participating in the unfolding of the larger world. What enables that participation is the pristine naked awareness spoken of in Patanjali's* Yoga Sutras. *As well, I am helped by what are called the* siddhis, *inaccurately thought to be special powers of an individual. However, the* siddhis *are not attainments – which is how they are often* *described. They are not something one can possess – they are a becoming and a process in which one's alignment makes participation possible. At times.*

Trylus: Are there obstacles?

Swann: *Yes, there are. But friends are close by. And, working together, obstacles can be overcome. Limitations can become opportunities as your poem "Sensible" makes clear.*

Trylus: [big smile]

§

Sensible

The falconer is blind
But he is not deterred by the lack
Of an external visual sense of perception.
It helps him hone his other senses.
Nor does he need to name those senses.

He raised his falcon from birth.
They work in concert
A concert of senses
Animal senses.
But perhaps there is something more.
One flies,
One does not – at least externally.
Internally, what are their worlds?
And how do they mesh?
The meshing of worlds:
This is friendship.[4]

§§§

9. Sardis Weaving

The Temple of Artemis at Sardis is weaving me in – weaving me into a story that I didn't realize must be told. Who tells these stories?

The high priestess sits, motionless, waiting for the goddess Artemis to manifest in awareness. A larger field of awareness must be shared through a synchronization of life-engendering frequencies. The goddess is more alive than the priestess, so only a narrow band can be shared, but it is enough for communication to pass in both directions.

The moon is full. Night is gathered all around. Candles burn and incense hangs richly through the vast and columned marble hall.

Priestess: Right reverence, what is your command?
Artemis: *Tonight, the fickle winds, tamed by my presence, have brought an interloper into this sacred precinct.*
Priestess: Is there danger?
Artemis: *It is very delicate.*
Priestess: In what way?
Artemis: *First, this entity is male.*
Priestess: [gasp]
Artemis: *Fear not. I have ensured that he is encased and can do no harm among us.*
Priestess: But why have you ordered the winds to bring him here?

Artemis: *He is here to learn. He comes from a time of darkness where almost no light shines, from a time when this temple lies in ruins, from a time when the earth has been laid waste and burns.*

Priestess: How could that be?

Artemis: *I see it clearly and I mourn. We must help.*

Priestess: But he is encased.

Artemis: *Yes, but he is not impervious. We must try.*

He must stand at the altar beside you, on your left.

Hold his hand.

Priestess: Must I?

Artemis: *You really must. Such is my command.*

Priestess: His hand is dirty.

Artemis: *Bring water, rose petals, and myrrh. Wash him gently. Rein in your disgust and: Smile!*

Priestess: It is done.

Artemis: *The work begins.*

Look into his eyes as you pour the libation onto the altar stone.

Priestess: As I look, there is an ugly mixing of his energies and mine.

Artemis: *Steady. Steady now, my priestess. You are impregnated by my energies. The roughness of his energies can only be refined as you engage. But you must hold fast to what is true within you. Doubt not. Be firm, holy the firm.*

Priestess: I hear delicate notes as winds play the Aeolian harp[5] in our courtyard.

Artemis: *Yes, the wind, being under my command, also enters into this work of elevation.*

How does his hand feel now to you? And his eyes…

Priestess: He sits with me, righteously aligned. His hand less flabby, his eyes are…

Artemis: *Look deeply…*

Priestess: He wanders in high precincts. A falcon circles above him. The far-seeing falcon he must become.

Artemis: *Tell him what you see.*

Priestess: He shudders in disbelief.

Artemis: *Direct his eyes to see what you see.*

Priestess: How?

Artemis: *Never mind that you don't know, just do it. Gently.*

Priestess: Now we share the same vision. He tells me so. Clearly.

Artemis: *Feel now what it is you share, what is between the two of you. It is love, but very delicate because it must remain chaste and pure. Tell him so. Demand his agreement.*

Priestess: He says he agrees, but I hear a wavering in his voice.

Artemis: *Kneel. Both of you. Kneel.*

On the nape of the neck, each of you feels the touch of my hand.

Nothing now can ever be the same, for either of you. Nor for the world.

It is done.

A great work has been accomplished.

Priestess: I hear the heavenly cohort sing, "Hail, and farewell."

Artemis: *The entity has been returned to his time, chastened and alive. May he find his way through the world in love.*

§§§

10. A Storied Land

The Blue Mosque

It is nearly an hour's walk from my room in Istanbul's Pera Palas Hotel to the Blue Mosque. It is rumored that it was in room 411 of this hotel that Agatha Christie wrote *Murder on the Orient Express*. A mysterious key was found hidden under the floorboards of this room. Was it related somehow to her 10-day disappearance and apparent loss of all memory of who she was?

I cross the bridge over the waterway called "The Golden Horn," an inlet of the Bosphorus Strait that separates the European and Asian parts of the city of Istanbul. Besides the Blue Mosque, the other places I visit – Hagia Sophia, the Topkapi Palace Museum – are also on the European side.

Dutifully, I take off my shoes and enter.

Once inside, the force of what meets me is more than enough to deprive me of all memory of who I am.

Without penetrating very far into the building, I quickly find a spot where I can sink to my knees and sit on my heels. Something in me understands that I must remain motionless and just absorb. No one interrupts me – unlike at the Dome of the Rock Mosque in Jerusalem where a guard, noticing me become still and motionless, angrily says to me, "No praying!"

What is this force, this pervasive power? The vast interior space is full to the brim – every corner, every niche.

It is a force but it isn't pushy. It is very steady.

Why can I not recognize the part within me that perceives this force? It is neither visual nor auditory although both of these senses seem on high alert.

I remain sitting on my knees so long I can barely walk afterwards. Once walking, I walk on and on through the city until long after dark, returning late to the hotel.

How can it be that I feel this force so clearly still as I write about it now nearly 50 years later?

The night is warm:
Below the Bosphorus
A cool "under-river" flows.

In the mosque
The silence is so deep
It hurts.

Am I to be found?
So it would seem.
Rejoice, little man.

Blue Mosque Interior, Istanbul.
Reprinted with permission from the Keskin postcard archive of the Suna Kıraç Library, Koç University, Istanbul.

§

Konya

The young man near me on the long bus ride from Istanbul to Konya drops his copy of the Koran. Picking it up from the floor, he kisses it to apologize for his lack of awareness. Awareness of what is holy – a perception almost totally lacking in the Occidental World.

My journey to Konya is to attend a public performance of the Mevlevi dervishes' turning dance. From the time of Atatürk's coming to power in the 1920s, the dervish orders, formerly very powerful both politically and spiritually, were brutally suppressed. For that reason, the performance is presented as a "tourist attraction," held in a high school gymnasium with a hardwood floor painted with basketball court designs. The ceiling however is hung with fabric for the occasion and that helps both the impression and perhaps also the sound. I choose to attend the performance on December 17, 1971 – the 698th anniversary of the death of Mevlana (Our Master) Jalaluddin Rumi whose son Sultan Veled and followers began the Mevlevi dervish order in Konya in 1312.

The reed
Cries out in longing
For its reed-bed.

It is hollow
As are we:
Until the beloved comes.

Voices of men
Blend with the voice of the ney:
Turning to return.

My heart
Is turned
To love.

I return to my little hotel that is not the Pera Palas, still struggling to know where the dervishes have taken me. It is elsewhere and yet it is right here. The sensation is similar to looking for something and not being able to see it even though it is right in front of you.

My room has a toilet and washbasin but no shower so a couple of times in my week-long stay I venture out to the *hamam* (steam bath.) Big adventure. Not just steam. Two attendants scrub you down with soapy water and a rough cloth. Seeing layers of skin slough off. Then you recline in a little room to get served sweet Turkish tea. Renovated and restored. Alive.

Konya is located near the southern edge of the central Anatolian Plateau at an altitude of over 3,000 feet. So in December there is ice and snow, wind, and bitter cold. I learn that one of the city's mayors fell and died on the city hall steps because no one had cleared them of ice.

At the time of this visit I was impressed but bemused – not really clear about what I was feeling. Writing about it now, years later, it is clearer. For the spectator of the ceremony, the whirling dance is a spectacle; for the participant it is a possible entry point to another world.

The conical hats (*sikke*) the dervishes wear symbolize tombstones or death to the worldly self, and the flowing black cloak the burial shroud. Each tomb has a *sikke* placed at its head and is draped with an elaborately decorated shroud. The impenetrable but exquisitely beautiful calligraphic Arabic script in various styles is present everywhere throughout the place.

This closeup of an autumn flower from our garden resonates with my visit to Rumi's tomb. The image reminds me of Gurdjieff's response when he was asked why he kept the curtains closed during the day in his Paris apartment. Pointing at his chest he indicated that it is the inner sun we seek, not the sun in the sky above us.

Like the Blue Mosque, the space in the building housing Rumi's tomb and the tombs of other important successors feels very full. It is more a gentle pervasiveness rather than a force – like the penetrating quality of pure love. The urge to dwell in the House of the Lord.

Coming to rest
In welcoming arms
That hold without holding.

Rumi's Draped Sarcophagus
Reprinted with permission from the Keskin postcard archive of the Suna Kıraç Library, Koç University, Istanbul.

§

Receiving and Transmitting

Becoming quiet and returning to that fullness of feeling, I sense the sun – the sun within me. Shadows are chased away by bright illumination. Impelled by forces beyond my ken, I decide I must speak with Mevlana.

Trylus: Much of the poetry you wrote in Persian has now spread around the world in the uncivilized, barbaric language we call "English." Since you also used Arabic, Turkish, and Greek, maybe you have some advice for those of us who struggle to convey, nearly eight hundred years later, what we experience of your presence and your understanding.

Rumi: Each language has its soul. Just as you must be close to your soul to receive from Above, so too you must be close to the soul of your language to write truth.

Trylus: And the role of my body? It can be wild or fierce but its perceptions can be subtle and deep. How should I be toward it?

Rumi: Be kind, tolerant, but firm. Your body understands the difference between receiving and giving. The position of the two hands in our turning dance – the right receiving from Above, the left giving to what is Below – both are holy. Seeing this, even without entering into the dance, you are instructed. And if you can enter, with others, so much the better.

Trylus: And the music! Oh, the music! There seem to be many things awry with the world I currently inhabit but access to the music of the turning dance is available to me at a moment's notice regardless of where I reside. Unbelievable but true.

Rumi: Regardless of how it might be available to you, what is important is how it enters you and the action it sets in motion within you.

Trylus: Can you say more?

Rumi: It can cleanse and irrigate. But only if you are open and submit to its influence. It very much depends on you and your attitude in relation to it. Work with that. Be intelligent in your feelings.

Trylus: I feel blessed by your presence and by our exchange.

Rumi: As Virgil said, "*Amor vincit omnia.*" "Love conquers all."

§§§

11. The Legend of Uxmal

Uxmal (pronounced Ushmal and meaning three times) is an ancient Mayan city located 62 km south of Mérida, the capital of Yucatan State in Mexico. It was a dominant center around 900 CE.

An alternative interpretation of the meaning of the name, based on the pronunciation Uchmal, is "What is to come, the future." Tradition has it that Uxmal was an invisible city, built by magic. A dwarf king ruled it.

The most striking structure on the site is called the Pyramid of the Magician or the Pyramid of the Dwarf. The architecture is unique in that its edges are rounded.

Snakes and the planet Venus are important features of the decorative friezes on the extensive site and relate to the rain god Chaac.

Pyramid of the Magician, Uxmal

As I stand looking at this building on a hot and humid sunny day in June, there is a sense of expectancy. There is not a breath of air and only a few tourists are wandering around loosely. The expectancy seems to be in the stones and it pervades the whole place. Something is bound to be.

§

The Once and Future King

Legends come down to us
And they speak to us in words that are strong
and bright.
The phrase "The Once and Future King"
Is ringing now
Ringing in me deeply and with love.
How strange that it comes to me with such force,
Since I know very little about the legend.
There was a king named Arthur.
There was a sword called "Excaliber."
That's all I can remember as I write these words.

But maybe remembering detail is not the point,
Is not why I'm given these words:
"The Once and Future King."
Maybe it's because something that is strong
and glorious
Is destined to return.

Time is folded, we are told.
Folded so that the creases can touch.

And a dynamic play of forces means that change
is constant.
I am given this phrase and it brings me love.
Deep love.

How am I to be with the gift?
I hear the words,
"Open and embrace what you are given.
Do not question the 'how' of it.
Embrace it.
Be joyful
And rest assured
That it is what it needs to be."

The Once and Future King Returns.

§

I recall being told, "Don't be naïve." Something in me rises up and objects to the sentiments expressed in this poem that was given suddenly and unexpectedly. There is evidence of a violent and bloody history at Uxmal and in the whole region, is there not?

Well, yes there is. But then someone asks, "Why do the most powerful angels brandish a sword?"

What do I really understand? Do I really understand *anything*?

In the legends of Uxmal, the dwarf's mother was a sorceress who protected him from an arrogant king. The king proposed contests and ended up losing his life in the third and final contest, so the dwarf became king. But then he too became arrogant. He and the city fell into oblivion.

Open Milkweed Seed Pods

Milkweed seeds
About to be airborne.
Time chuckles.

A dwarf whispers in my ear,
"Don't think 'either/or,'
Think 'and'."

Love is a sorcery
Strong and glorious.
Brandishing angels smile.

§§§

12. Leonardo's "Salvator Mundi"

With some of the conversations I receive, as the intent to choose a particular subject is forming, several times I have been hit by the thought, "Do I dare choose that?" (Of course I don't really choose – I accept what I'm given.) More than any other case, this hesitation was true as I recently became acquainted with Leonardo da Vinci's painting of Jesus always referred to by its Latin title "Salvator Mundi" (Savior of the World). Wikipedia's article titled "Salvator Mundi (Leonardo)" has a small image and a long exposition of the painting's chequered history. The woman who restored it was deeply moved as her work progressed. She had to deal with physical damage to the painting's wooden panel as well as multiple layers of overpainting by people who thought they were improving the image. Let me begin by saying a few things about what struck me about this work.

The right hand, the hand that is blessing, is painted so vividly that it appears to emerge out of the painting towards the viewer. The face, in contrast, is painted as if it were slightly out of focus and the neck is so fuzzy that the face seems to float, detached, above it. The brow is shining, as is the exposed skin of the chest, shining like searchlights. The black background is uniform and unremitting. Given Leonardo's skill all this has to be deliberate – *and* meaningful.

Most intriguing of all is the completely transparent sphere in his left hand. Now Leonardo had studied and knew a great deal about light and optics. So then why did he paint this sphere as if it were hollow or incapable of refracting light? The folds of the garment behind it are undistorted. Speaking of light, notice that there are three points of light in or on the sphere. Notice too that the tips of the fingers on the left hand and the heel of that hand under the sphere are strongly illuminated. I see the illumination as coming from the hand that is blessing but maybe that's just me.

And lastly the eyes. They are partially hidden and yet they speak. As you engage with this painting (even in its form as a reproduction on a computer screen), you can *feel* a meeting is taking place. You can feel that you are facing a being whose presence is so high that the disparate elements of the painting are trembling because they cannot contain his immensity.

It is my intent in the following conversation to have an exchange with what and who is behind this image.

Trylus: As I engage, I feel that I am lifted out of myself and into myself at the same time. How can I bring what is worthy of this meeting?

Salvator: *You bring what and who you are. Nothing more, nothing less.*

Trylus: But at the same time something in me feels transformed.

Salvator: *You are not only you. You also are me. And everything else in the universe. But what you are noticing is taking place in your vision, in your awareness. No?*

Trylus: Yes. In my awareness.

Salvator: *Be conscious of your consciousness as you experience* *what you experience. More will then be possible for you. But do not do this with the thinking mind. Do it with pure awareness.*

Trylus: Why did you have Leonardo paint the sphere as being totally transparent?

Salvator: *Because there is nothing to see. It had to be clear that I am not holding a crystal ball, I am holding transparency. Sometimes you need to be aware of the container not the contained. Notice though the three points of light that live in total transparency, total purity. Allow that to speak to you.*

Trylus: I wondered if Leonardo wanted to say that the world is transparent to you.

Salvator: *Maybe he did, but of what importance is that to you?*

Trylus: Right.

As I look again at Leonardo's painting, as happened before, the various elements, hand, sphere, face, the eyes begin to quiver as if they are about to fly apart. What is this perception?

Salvator: *Allow that quivering to enter you. It is a quivering at the edge of life. It will help you be more alive.*

Trylus: I am skittish and you are utterly still. How can I move in the direction of stillness?

Salvator: *You are with me. Breathe. Breathe our contact into what and who you are. Breathe as you've never breathed before. Transparently.*

Trylus: I feel closer to the stillness and to you.

Salvator: *Yes, you are closer. But you will forget. Again and again you will forget.*

Trylus: Is there no remedy?

Salvator: *There are many remedies, none perfect. But in this case, I advise you to use Leonardo's gift as you have been doing. His work with me was an excellent collaboration. I asked him to paint the quivering joy at the edge of creation. And he did!*

Trylus: I will come back to it again and again.
Salvator: *Very well.*

§§§

13. The Grateful Stone

A dear friend of mine, Chantale, spoke to me recently about her 2007 trip to Peru. It was almost tragic because she fell ill, very ill, when visiting the Amazon region city of Tarapoto in the north. A shaman helped her recover and she felt it was also some kind of sign that, in spite of, or because of, her extreme fear of snakes, she encountered a snake that was all red, a light coral red – apparently a very rare species.

But the most mysterious part of the trip was her visit to one of a cluster of archeological sites near Cusco in what is called "The Sacred Valley." The principal one she visited is called "Amaru Marca Huasi" in the Quechua language of the Incas and literally means "snake village house." This site is also commonly called "El Templo de la Luna" (The Temple of the Moon). It is a naturally occurring cavern in the hillside, but it was added to and crafted with additional structures. Her visit took place on June 1st, 2007, just after her birthday on May 29th and immediately following her visit to Machu Picchu on May 30th. Chantale's guide said that the Temple was a place for meditation.

Venturing past the cavern's mouth, Chantale found inside a kind of alcove or niche to which she felt drawn. She stepped into it and stood facing out. Amazingly it was exactly her height of 5 foot 4 inches. Behind her, the stone was curved and fit her back perfectly. And there was just enough room at the sides for her arms to rest comfortably against her body.

Once positioned in this way, she was flooded by a feeling of deep peace – so deep in fact she had no desire to ever leave that spot. Of course, convention overruled that feeling as her companions insisted they move on to visit other places. But an unforgettable impression had been made.

One day recently, as the two of us were discussing this remarkable adventure, the idea arose from somewhere that Chantale should use the automatic writing skills she sometimes practiced to return to the site and find out more. Automatic writing is a type of channeling in which the writer enters a trance-like state and writes non-stop with no engagement of the mind. The channeler has no knowledge of the written content until afterwards she rereads what has come through.

Since our discussion and the automatic writing took place in French, I am providing an English translation here of what came through.

§

Chantale: [Addressing herself to the niche where she had been standing.]

What happened to me in this cavern?

Response: *I recognized you. You were here a long time ago. I was happy to see you again.*

Chantale: Who am I?

Response: *A warrior of light, a man who did a great deal for his people.*

[As an aside, Chantale comments to me that she has a very hard time imagining being in a man's body.]

Chantale: Are you sure I was a man?

Response: *A little. You weren't really either man or woman. For you, that didn't mean anything. You came here to help others with your great sensitivity. You gave them faith and hope.*

Chantale: What year was this?

Response: *1642. About 1642.*

Chantale: There was war?

Response: *Yes. The Spanish were invading us. But you were living in your joy. You came here to this cavern, to this niche to fill yourself with joy and then you would go and comfort the people of your village.*

Chantale: What was my name?

Response: *Maripusack Krum*

Chantale: How did I die?

Response: *Drowned.* [At this point Chantale is shown an image of a lake where someone is sinking into the water while singing and looking out to the Sacred Valley mountains. Like a boat gently sinking. This image is very,

very strong for Chantale and evokes an incident at age six in her current life when she almost drowned. Then too she was at great peace until someone "rescued" her.]

Chantale: Was it suicide?

Response: *No. Well, a little. You were not afraid of death. You were ready and had done a great deal for your brothers and sisters, for your people. You were ready to leave. You left immersed in joy.*

When you returned to the cavern, you brought to life once again all the joy. I have been needing you for so long.
Thank you.

Chantale: You brought me great peace. When I was there in that niche, I felt at home.

Response: *That's because you were at home. You were the one who built the structures in this cavern. What you did was to meditate so much here that the walls were imprinted with you. You entered straight into that imprint when you walked into the cavern.*

Chantale: What is the message?

Response: *Find your joy once again.*

Chantale: I must find my joy?

Response: *You are so sad in your current life. This sadness is not your soul and is not your karma. You are made to be joyful. And you are very powerful when you are joyful. You can do things that you can't even imagine. Just as Maripusack Krum did. You ought to die as he did – joyful and singing. Sing. Chantale, your name.*

Chantale: Thank you.

A note on Chantale's name:

In its sound, the name Chantale is close to "chanter" which means to sing in French. Etymologically, Chantale in the Occitan language of southern France means "stone."

The last three sentences of the response in French are:

Tu dois mourir comme lui dans la joie en chantant. Chante. Chantale, ton nom.

Note the repetition: chantant chante chantale.

§§§

14. A Question of Eyes

Silos are used to store grain and they are vital in hard times. Do we know where our silos are? Are they safe from decay and pests?

When wisdom is in short supply, can we find its silo? Instinctively, we know that without it we are at risk.

Suddenly, I feel impelled to ask for help from Ts'ang Chieh, the legendary inventor of Chinese writing.

Trylus: When there is a need, how can we go about finding a source of supply?

Ts'ang Chieh: *Of course the artist who painted me with three sets of eyes was taking a chance in his daring image on the west wall of Yongle Palace,*[6] *but his point remains valid. You do need different sets of eyes. The eyes of body, mind, and heart are one set that is fundamental.*

Trylus: In the image I see humility and effort. Reverence too.

Ts'ang Chieh: *That's right, he captured that as well – three other essential elements.*

Trylus: I am concerned that access may need to be across time and through worlds.

Ts'ang Chieh: *Yes, ancestral wisdom is essential to life in the present.*

Trylus: Memory of that seems to have vanished from my world.

Ts'ang Chieh: *So it may seem, but once again it is a question of eyes. Ancestral wisdom cannot be lost, cannot be destroyed. Human lives can appear to be lost, can appear to be destroyed, but that is illusion as well.*

You evoked me. How was that done?

Trylus: Your image came into my mind.

Ts'ang Chieh: *Just so. Why did my image come into your mind?*

Trylus: I have no idea. It came out of nowhere.

Ts'ang Chieh: *So it may seem. But what I see is that it arose from a deeply felt need in you.*

Trylus: Yes. There is a deeply felt need for such a source. My own resources are woefully inadequate for what I face.

Ts'ang Chieh: *No, no. Not woefully. They are sufficient, otherwise this dialogue would not be taking place.*

Trylus: When I began with the image of silos, I had a vision of them arcing across more than one world.

Ts'ang Chieh: *The comet Neowise is present just now in your skies to remind you of the need for a very large orbit. Don't limit your orbit to the one world you know. Your orbit, your silo, must extend to other worlds as well. You remember – the one you visited with Henry that had an entirely different sense of order.*

Trylus: Yes, I remember how different that was.

Ts'ang Chieh: *Remember and apply that to the issues you currently face.*

Trylus: It's as if I can see now without agitation.

Ts'ang Chieh: *Yes. And that was only one example. The*

number of worlds is vast.

Trylus: I sense a feeling connection between us.

Ts'ang Chieh: [smiling] *How could there not be? You know... We go back a long way.*

Trylus: I don't know that but I feel that.

Ts'ang Chieh: *Even better. Till the next time then.*

Trylus: Yes, till the next time.

§§§

15. Shape Shifting
The Planet Venus

Over the series of trips I make to Mexico, a friendship develops with the American man, Jon, with whom I had shared a room at the retreat center I attended on my first trip in 2013. Jon and his wife Estela run a cooking school called "Mexican Home Cooking" in the city of Tlaxcala which is located a couple of hours by road south-east of Mexico City.

On my initial visit to his home, Jon takes me to the nearby archeological site named "Cacaxtla" in San Miguel del Milagro. This site is known for its murals created over one thousand years ago. One in particular strikes me forcibly. The images on display in the site's museum are reproductions of the original murals, but they have the advantage of being very clear. Amazingly, the colors in the originals in the nearby site are just as vibrant as what we see in the reproductions. The figure included here is associated with the planet Venus and its related god Quetzalcoatl, the plumed serpent or quetzal serpent who is the god of wisdom, learning, and books.

Cacaxtla Shape Shifter

What do I take on?
A color?
I hear the gods whispering.

And the Earth trembles.
We are here
So brief a time.

Don't deny
Your true sense of being.
Honor it.

§

La Malinche

Each time I visit Jon in Tlaxcala, I marvel at the stunning view his property has of the dormant volcanic mountain called "La Malinche" or "Matlalcueyetl" in the Nahuatl language of the Aztecs.

La Malinche at Dawn

On October 28, 2017, I finally get to realize a long-time dream and, with the help of a young friend of Jon's, I manage to climb almost to the top of this amazing mountain. Since Tlaxcala is on the high central plain of Mexico, the altitude of the city is already 7,000 feet. The mountain itself rises to 14,000 feet. I know this is not going to be a sensible thing to do since I have not trained first and I am about to turn 77. However, a part of me knows I have to attempt it. No arguing and no turning back. We begin from a kind of "base camp" with parking and park buildings.

A thistle we see near the beginning seems to symbolize the exquisite and beautiful nature of the climb:

Repeatedly, I have to stop to catch my breath, something the young man with me does not have to do. A reminder of the forces that lie dormant beneath our feet are the deep gouges that look like rivers of stone.

Heights beckon.
The mountain speaks.
And its flowers answer.

As we stop to eat the lunches we have brought, we notice we are at the edge of the vegetation. Further up there is only shifting gravel and stones. There is no one in sight. A particular quiet descends.

And a communication begins.

I am on something. Something that is not inert. Something that has both feelings and intelligence. And I am here through the agency of its good graces. It allows me to be here. The idea that the choice of being here is mine now seems ridiculous. Something decided that I would be here. Prodded, my mind worked out certain practical details. But fundamentally this something is in charge because it is a higher order of intelligence.

It is not speaking but it does smile at my curious human deliberations.

Its smile is also acknowledging that I have loved this mountain from the first moment I saw it in this current life. My love is now being returned. Not in words but in an embrace. I am held. I am cradled. I am rocked.

These moments of perception do not last but, once perceived, neither do they seem to leave. It is as if they have their own dwelling place inside me.

Following a short rest after lunch we begin again to climb. It is hard going. We get up some distance above the little bump on the north side just below the top, but we decide to abandon getting to the very top and we turn back in order to get to the car before dark. The descent is slow and painful because my right knee is in trouble. When we reach the car I can barely walk and I almost collapse a few feet from the car. Once back at Jon's I need two people supporting me to get to my room.

Thank goodness for the energy work I do and can do for myself. The next day I have no pain and I am walking normally.

But what is it that I have done?

In my heart
There is a mountain now:
A mountain of fierce love.

§

In Mexico you never know who or what you might suddenly encounter. Here is the only surviving pre-Conquest stone carving of Matlalcueyetl (The Nahuatl name of the volcano La Malinche), built into the wall of the church in San Sabastián Atlahapa near Tlaxcala. The word Matlalcueyetl very appropriately means green skirt. Matlalki is green. Cuecueyotl is sphere, which in traditional knowledge refers to the chakra system. There is also a suggestion of radiance and splendor.

Focus on this image and then allow your eyes to de-focus slightly. The image will begin to tremble behind your eyes. Let it. What does Matlalcueyetl have to say to you?

Matlalcueyetl (La Malincha)

§

Pulque Mediates

In the clutter of life, one sometimes stumbles on the miraculous.

My friend Alan in Mexico City has been saying I ought to try the Mexican drink called "*pulque*." It is a slightly alcoholic (4 to 5 %) fermented drink made from the juice of the agave cactus. It has a skim milky color and a sour taste. I have been avoiding trying it because someone said it was a bit like okra, a bit slimy, and I hate okra. It is a kind of home brew that has never been commercialized so there is a wide range in how competently it gets produced. Someone has theorized that when the conquering Europeans introduced beer, pulque got sidelined.

One day, as Alan and I are out on a road trip, he exclaims, "There's a great pulque establishment here! Let's stop and try it." I was trapped and knew that I would have to at least try it.

Pulque lunch

I say that I want the unflavored kind so I can actually taste it – not the kind that has fruit juice added.

Here we are in the clutter of life, French fries, sauces, some chapulines which I like (fried grasshoppers). I take one small sip of the unflavored pulque and immediately I begin to cry.

The feeling of longing is intense: it has been so very long that I have not tasted this drink. Oh, so very long.

An avalanche of images washes over me. Ceremonial

feathered headdresses, masked faces, brilliant colors, drums, and song.

It is only a moment, a brief moment that does not linger – although the feelings take some time to dissipate. Gradually I return to myself and explain as best I can to Alan what has just taken place.

Much later I learn that in traditional native society, before the Conquest, pulque was a drink that only senior, high-ranking people were allowed to drink. If others drank it, the penalty was death. Traces of it have been found in ceremonial areas of the Templo Major in Mexico City.

Who am I?
I am all
That I have been, am, and will be.

§

Trylus: I need to know more. Something in the taste of those times needs to return, now, to complete a certain understanding. And something else, now, hinges on this completion.

Speak to me, pulque.

Pulque: *I can only whisper.*

Trylus: No matter. Let us try.

Pulque: *A woman stands before you. She is proud and resplendent. You, a warrior, are equally proud and resplendent. You have never met before. Priests have arranged this meeting. Something is said about destiny. Something is said about the gods. Offerings are made. Rituals are duly performed.*

Trylus: And where do you come into this?

Pulque: *As you look into each other's eyes, you taste.*

Trylus: Taste pulque?

Pulque: *Yes, but not only. It is more subtle than that.*

Trylus: I don't understand.

Pulque: *It's a question of essence. My essence, your essence, her essence.*

Trylus: Ah.

Pulque: *You say, "Ah." But you are not entering into the moment in the way you need to do.*

Trylus: …

Pulque: *Yes, that is better. Taste. Taste who you are, who she is, who I am. There is a blessed trinity here you missed last time. Your warriorness rose up. "I am in charge," it said." You ceased to taste. The woman shrank back, imperceptibly. Fear entered.*

Trylus: I'm following you.

Pulque: *Now let us engage in the repair.*

Enter once again into this scene. Focus on the taste. Focus on the subtlety.

Trylus: There begins to be a blending of essences.

Pulque: *You begin to see. But you do not yet understand that "who you are" is changing. The priest who is presiding knows and follows the movement of transformation.*

Trylus: But I am powerful. My power is faltering. This will not do.

Pulque: *Do not make this mistake again. Look up. What is above you?*

Trylus: An eagle. Circling. Suddenly I am looking through his eyes. I am looking down.

Pulque: *Yes, a new perspective. What do you taste?*

Trylus: I taste a circling. A blending of these three.

Pulque: *It is for a higher purpose, a purpose from On High.*

Trylus: It is not clear.

Pulque: *It cannot be clear to the person you are still. You must allow the circling to take you to who your destiny says you must become.*

Trylus: But then I die!

Pulque: *It is a death. But it is also a resurrection.*

Trylus: This is something I cannot fight and win.

Pulque: *Precisely. This is something you ease into. And you have help. The woman will help you this time. Last time you prevented her from helping you. Look into her eyes right now.*

Trylus: A circling. An eagle. An inner circling. I do not understand.

Pulque: *Patience. Remember I am your friend. But only when I am swallowed with respect. You need time now to absorb and digest what has happened up to now. It is no small thing.*

Trylus: I bow to your savor.

§§§

16. The Smoking Mirror

From Central America, Tezcatlipoca, Lord of Days, gifts us the image of the smoking mirror and four coded directives. Hold the mirror's image firmly in mind and say these words resonantly aloud:

I am the invisible.
I am the night.
I am the smile.
I am the wall.[7]

Trylus: Speak to me mirror, speak.

Mirror: *Where there is smoke, there is fire. Walk through the embers. Banish fear.*

Trylus: I enter walking, walking slowly. But I do not see. Smoke billows. My eyes are painful. I ask your help.

Mirror: *I give you a scepter to hold in your right hand. And a diamond in your left. Hold both with a firmness that is not tense.*

Trylus: My vision clears. I see the hills and valleys now. I listen to the mountain stream. What is this land?

Mirror: *This land is you. Have you forgotten that what you approached is a mirror?*

Trylus: Yes, I had forgotten the mirror.

Mirror: *What do you see ahead?*

Trylus: I see a child – a towhead, carefree child.

Mirror: *Approach him.*

Trylus: He seems to recognize me.

Mirror: *Of course. How could he not?*

Trylus: We run through sunshine and through song. Our joy is boundless.

Mirror: *And who approaches now?*

Trylus: A beggar. Bent, disheveled, and clothed in rags.

Dirty. He looks at us imploringly.

Mirror: *And?*

Trylus: I touch his head with the scepter and his figure turns to dust – a pile of dust from which there spirals up a crested lark speaking at heaven's gate.

Mirror: *Close your eyes and remain very still.*

Trylus: The ground beneath my feet is shaking now.

Mirror: *The god of this mirror approaches. Open your eyes and look steadily at his approaching form. He wants to see who has disturbed his slumber. Centuries have passed without this threshold being crossed.*

Quickly now, without haste, expand yourself so your size is commensurate with his. And fix your gaze upon him. Unwavering and prepared.

Trylus: We are face to face. The ground is shaking still. I hold the scepter firm. Blue lightning sparks off it as our eyes meet and penetrate each other's depths.

Mirror: *Say now what you have been given to say.*

Trylus: I am that I am.

Mirror: *And what is his response?*

Trylus: He says the same: I am that I am.

Mirror: *And then?*

Trylus: We begin to laugh. We laugh and laugh. Mountains tremble with the sound.

Mirror: *What gesture now?*

Trylus: I extend my left hand toward him with the diamond on my open palm.

Mirror: *What is his response?*

Trylus: He does the same. On his left palm there is a diamond of equal size and brilliance. Held in proximity they create a shower of scintillating lights that spread out far and wide.

Mirror: *And then?*

Trylus: Once again we laugh. We laugh and laugh. And once again the mountains thunderously resound.

Then a moment of stillness. We face each other in the silence. We smile.

A final warm embrace and turning sharply we stride off, each upon his holy path, striding into night.

Mirror: *The pole star shines.*

§§§

17. The Part That Knows

I address my guardian angel.

Trylus: When in the later stages of a life one stumbles across major aspects of that life that were an enduring fantasy or never-to-happen dreams – how to be in the face of that?

Angel: *Be kind.*

Trylus: But I ache.

Angel: *Hold the ache at the back of the head, in the hollow called the nape of the neck and breathe into it. Breath by breath. Let the sour melancholy turn to the taste of summer rain on the face, a face upheld.*

Trylus: The space is larger now, inside.

Angel: *Now, in that space, find and relish those aspects of the life, so far, that were grand. And you know very well there have been many grand moments. The mountains you climbed, the oceans you crossed.*

Trylus: True. Yes, this is true.

Angel: *Place this truth where you can find it more easily next time. On that small shelf, just there.*

Trylus: I'll bookmark it in my mind.

Angel: *That's fine so long as you remember to check your bookmarks once in a while. You need to remember to stop long enough, often enough, for that to take place.* [smile]

Trylus: And the time that remains? How to be in the face of that mystery?

Angel: *Be kind to the part that does not know, even though another part does know. Don't spend so much time in the part that does not know. Trust the part that knows.*

Trylus: But that part often does not speak.

Angel: *Why would it need to speak if it knows?*

Trylus: Erh… But I am a writer. I have a love affair with words.

Angel: *It's not a matter of this or that; it's this* and *that.*

Trylus: Oh.

Angel: *Listen to the part that does not speak. And write from that listening.*

Trylus: My mind spins.

Angel: *Let it spin. That's what it was designed to do. But you don't have to spin with it. Remain observant and aware. You must not die before your time. Relish the aliveness that you know very well is there.*

Trylus: I breathe easier now.

Angel: *As do I.*

Reaching for God

§§§

18. An Area of Sacred Forgiveness

We are told repeatedly by the wise,
"Look inside not outside
For what is precious."

Therefore:
I must find within my core,
An ally who will craft there,
In secret,
A treasure chest of acacia wood,
Rectangular and sized to match my stature.
This chest, designed to house the power of my star,
Is to be plated with gold,
Inside and out.
Perhaps this will take some time.
Time to reflect, and learn, and grow.

On the flat top of this coffer,
An area must be delineated
Matching the chest in length and breadth, and
Dedicated for sacred forgiveness.
This space will be graced by the presence of
two golden angels,
One at either end,
Facing each other and the space between them,
With their outstretched wings raised
Over this hallowed ground.
Their presence and their gesture must be earned.

My heart and mind must understand
That I carry forward now,
Poised,
In secret,
A vital chest, wrought in gold,
Wherever I may roam.

Gold Enclosed with Azure

§§§

19. There Is a Tide…

There is a tide in the affairs of men
Which, taken at the flood, leads on to fortune
Omitted, all the voyage of their life
Is bound in shallows and in miseries.
On such a full sea are we now afloat,

And we must take the current when it serves,
Or lose our ventures.

Shakespeare, *Julius Caesar*, Act 4, Scene 3, Lines 218-224.

As the fourth world ends and the fifth world begins, the tides are stronger and much more apparent. Mesmerized by what is being swept away, how can we awaken to the budding possibilities of what is being born?

I address Pakal, Mayan ruler of Palenque, 615-683 CE, whose name means "Resplendent Shield."

Trylus: Pakal. You travel and mediate between worlds. Your image has been preserved through the art you commissioned. That art itself is a help. Respectfully, I ask your help for our time of transition between the fourth and fifth worlds. You knew this transition was coming not so very long after your reign.

Pakal: *What is dead is being swept away. It is a death that had already been begun in my time. I give you my shield as protection while you move through this time. Be careful to align yourselves with what is alive and growing. Let the dead fall away.*

Trylus: You are generous and I am honored. Can you say more?

Pakal: *There is a specific vibration to which you need to be aligned. You do this by listening, careful listening. You will recognize this vibration by its quality. You must do this because the level of distraction is high, but also because of what the vibration has to convey. It is a harbinger. Listen both to the base vibration and to the overtones. Do this alone. Do this for yourself. Your action will then emanate to others.*

Trylus: The night seems darker now.

Pakal: *Fear not. These are nights of power. Heaven is looking down. Although you are in darkness, look up and feel the look that descends upon you. This is grace, benevolent grace with all her gentleness in flower and in song.*

Trylus: I am reminded of al-Khidr, the green man, who

appears unexpectedly right at the critical turning points of life.

Pakal: *I know him well. Remember to not question his actions; do not question what he does and doesn't do. He sees much further than you can understand. Be honored that you are in his presence and that you walk on with bravery and steadfastness through the night until you see the dawn.*

Trylus: Pakal, you were the inheritor of sophisticated technical knowledge such as the calendar that was superior to the one being used in Europe during your era. Our civilization suffers from an imbalance or a split between the technical and the spiritual. Perhaps such a split will appear bizarre to you…

Pakal: *Not only bizarre – it is meaningless. Technology that does not interact with and serve the cosmic forces is a failed technology.*

Trylus: I fear that in the chaos of this transition between worlds we could lose all of our technology. Wouldn't this be a disaster?

Pakal: *What it would be is not anything you have the power to affect. All of that is determined by levels far above your civilization. Just as I see that my people now are destitute when it comes to technology, your civilization may suffer the same fate. I glimpse that it won't, but your future is still in the process of being formed. What is to come depends on how you are now in the chaos. Hold fast to your links to those in levels above you. Breathe deeply.*

§§§

20. Sacred Space

How is a sacred space known? Through what faculty of perception do I become aware that a space is sacred? We may become aware of it because our voices become softer or hushed. But that is how we react to it, not how we perceive it.

The greatest architects and musicians knew something about this. Walking into twelfth century cathedrals such as Chartres in France or into spaces like the Blue Mosque in Istanbul, there is an immediate response in a certain part of ourselves. Unless we are too encrusted or distracted to feel.

Perhaps this faculty is what makes us uniquely human.

I address my angel.

Trylus: It is clear that this faculty of perception, the perception of the sacred, exists but how can I become instructed in its use?

Angel: *Look more deeply and more carefully at the natural world around you. Which element you choose does not matter. Pick something and bring yourself into resonance – a resonance between what you call this faculty and the chosen element, or the chosen being. As you progress in knowing this element you will be exercising that faculty. As the haiku poet Bashō said, "Learn about pines from the pine; learn about bamboo from the bamboo. Don't follow in the footsteps of the old poets, seek what they sought."*[8] *This is a way to begin.*

Trylus: Much around me is of human construction and it seems that it doesn't have the same possibilities.

Angel: *Those things have possibilities too. You can know something by its absence. There is a knowing through longing for* *what is missing. Remember your 1960s haiku:*

The wind:
Forced to blow
On concrete, steel, and glass.

Trylus: I see.

Angel: *Yes, you see a little. But there is more.*

Trylus: What am I missing?

Angel: *What you see is affected by where in yourself you are looking from. If you stand behind a mountain you won't see the valley and its river on its other side. Sometimes it's not a mountain it's a cage with carefully constructed bars that you have fashioned with your own hands.*

Trylus: I feel trapped.

Angel: *Yes, you* are *trapped. But you may be able to step aside. Even a step or two can change your perspective. You may see the beginnings of a mountain path. Study your inner landscape carefully. Avoid assuming you know what is there in your inner world.*

Trylus: Is there something else you can add?

Angel: *Yes. What you began with. Space.*

Trylus: Space?

Angel: *As you study, it is important to sense that you have walked into a much larger sacred space. Your study takes place in a cosmic cathedral. Feel its infinite expanse as you work. You may not get to this right away, but if you persist it will be there around you.*

Trylus: Sometimes, I've had a sense of that space in my meditations.

Angel: *Yes. You are there only when you become more concentrated, more compact, less scattered or diffuse. Generally, you flicker.*

Study the faces of some of the famous aboriginal Indian chieftains of previous centuries and you may be able to see what is lacking in you.

Trylus: Anything more?

Angel: *Yes, the sacred space is recognized by its light. It is an uncreated light, light before it manifests. It can be seen with your inner eye.*

That is all. We have done all that can be done just now.

Do not think about these words. Reserve a quiet place for them in your heart and they will flower.

§§§

21. Links

The word "link" is used frequently in our times but do we really know what it is that we do when we link, when we connect to something?

I was just told, "Hold fast to your links to those in levels above you. Breathe deeply."

How is such a link fostered and maintained? How is it even made or established in the first place?

I address my angel.

Trylus: I am floundering and confused. Please help me be clear.

Angel: [smiling] *You seem to think that all links are made of the same substance, but of course they are not.*

Trylus: It never occurred to me to think of what they are made.

Angel: *Indeed.*

Trylus: My link with you… Of what is it made?

Angel: [smiling still] *That is very hard to say because your language has such limited ways of speaking of the substance of love. It has infinite shades and densities of substantiality. As I increase its concentration can you feel a change?*

Trylus: I am close to fainting away.

Angel: *Steady. Steady on.*
And when for a moment I stop its flow?

Trylus: I am destitute. I am dead.

And then when the moment ends once again I breathe and I shine.

Angel: *And now the substance of what comes from you to me. Increase it now.*

Trylus: Erh… I'm not sure where to begin.

Angel: *Well, it's not something to think about, is it? It begins with an opening in the heart. But then there must be a modulation. Modulation is the only word I can find. You must modulate the frequency so that it can reach me here where I dwell and have my existence.*

Trylus: I have no idea how to do that.

Angel: *Not true. You do have some idea. But you need to refine that idea and work with it. You need practice. It would seem that you have not been all that interested in your connection with me.*

Trylus: [blush]

Angel: *Now you're reducing the intensity instead of increasing it.*

Trylus: Sorry.

Angel: *Don't be sorry. Just take note and make an adjustment.*

Yes. Like that. Better now. A little better. At least it's in the right direction.

Don't try. Don't push. It needs gentleness.

Yes, that's right. It's even better now.

Trylus: Where would I be without you?

Angel: *Back perhaps in that river in the nether regions where it was arranged from Above that I would take your hand and pull you up. The will coming from Above is also part of the substance of our link.*

Trylus: Are there other elements as well?

Angel: *Many and various. But it would be of no use to enumerate them just now. Be content and foster what you have learned today. Don't let your laziness and your failures pull you down. Bring your attention to the link that you feel. Honor it and it will honor you.*

§§§

22. An Ocean of Printing

The year is 1232. Six thousand volumes of Buddhist scripture carved on wooden blocks, vital to the spiritual life of the Kingdom of Korea, burn in a fire during incursions by invading armies. What would you do? And how?

Emptiness is form
Form is emptiness
Says the Heart Sutra.

And yet…
And yet…
How can the heart not regret.

Drop regret.
Pick up the pieces.
Hold your head high.

Does King Gojong sense a national lack of spiritual resolve, an incarnate flabbiness that has given rise to the devastating invasions? Whatever his motivation, he masterfully sets about making a correction to the forces at play in his country. Thousands of craftsmen and scholars are assembled to produce, in twelve years beginning in 1237, what is now known as the Tripitaka Koreana, a version of the Buddhist scriptures considered to be error-free and more complete than any other compilation.

The result: 81,258 carved wooden blocks of birch, measuring 24 cm (10 inches) by 70 cm (28 inches), each weighing three to four kg (seven to nine pounds) and carrying 23 lines of text with 14 characters per line for a total of 52,830,152 characters. Don't forget that each character has to be carved in reverse, in mirror image, in order to print "right way around." And some of the Chinese characters (*hanja*) used in Korean writing can be incredibly complex as you can see in the Heart Sutra sample below.

And now, how to ensure they remain safely stored? Soak

the uncarved blocks in seawater for three years, boil them in salt water and let them dry in a shady and windy spot for another three years. Once they are carved, coat them with a lacquer that is poisonous to bugs and encase them in metal frames to prevent warping.

Soak and dry.
Prepare the mind
This way as well.

The mind needs space
For the wind
To blow through.

Now, where to safely store these records? In 1398, the woodblocks are moved to specially constructed storage halls built within the temple complex named Haeinsa (해인사, 海印寺) in Gayasan (가야산, 伽倻山) National Park. The first temple built on this site was constructed in 802 CE. "Haeinsa" means "Ocean of Printing Temple."

The storage halls are positioned on the highest point of land in the temple complex in such a way they are never exposed to direct sunlight and are protected from prevailing winds. The clay floors are filled with charcoal, calcium oxide, salt, lime, and sand, which reduce humidity when it rains by absorbing excess moisture which is then retained to humidify the dry winter months. Ample windows are designed to maximize ventilation and regulate temperature.

In 1970, an experiment is conducted by moving test blocks to a modern storage facility. The blocks begin to mildew so the project is dropped.

In the Wikipedia article entitled "Haeinsa," there is a nice image of the storage halls captioned "Tripitaka Koreana woodblocks at Haeinsa."

The storage buildings have survived seven serious fires and a near-bombing in which a pilot who was ordered to bomb the temple in the Korean War disobeyed the command because he remembered there was something priceless there.

The main hall of the complex, the "Hall of Great Silence and Light" (대적광전, 大寂光殿), is dedicated to Vairocana, he who dwells in ever tranquil light.

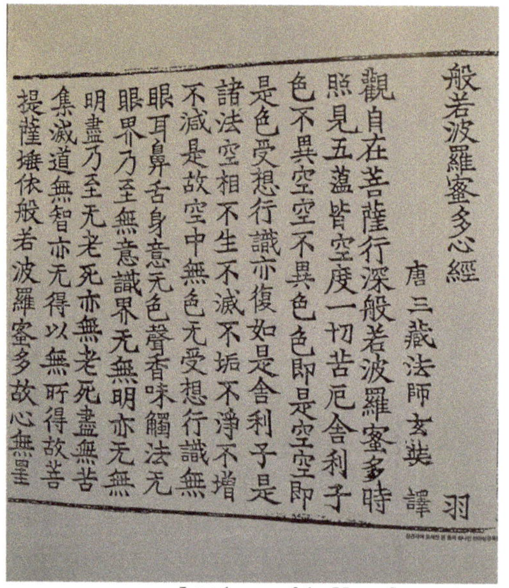

般若波羅蜜多心經
唐三藏法師玄奘 譯 羽
觀自在菩薩行深般若波羅蜜多時
照見五蘊皆空度一切苦厄舍利子
色不異空空不異色色即是空空即
是色受想行識亦復如是舍利子是
諸法空相不生不滅不垢不淨不增
不減是故空中無色无受想行識無
眼耳鼻舌身意无色聲香味觸法无
眼界乃至無意識界无無明亦无無
明盡乃至无老死亦無老死盡無苦
集滅道無智亦无得以無所得故菩
提薩埵依般若波羅蜜多故心無罣

Initial page of the Heart Sutra printed from its Haeinsa woodblock

"Sit," I Am Told

At 3 am
Sit in the Hall of Great Silence and Light.
The sound of gentle autumn rain
Helps quiet the mind.
Feel how Vairocana's ever tranquil light
Steadies awareness and resolve.
The voice of the wind in the pines
Speaks of the breathing planet
Supporting all of terrestrial life.
Taste the kinship that casts no ripples
Through the depths of silence
Behind all things.

Know
The 10,000 things
Are one.

§§§

23. Spirit Stones

Ise Rocks Bright. Photo: Ron Balamuth

The photograph of this site on the south-west coast of Japan in Mie Prefecture struck me with great force when it was sent to me by a friend who was visiting there a couple of years ago. And it has continued to work away in me until yesterday when I remembered it and felt an urgent need to include it here.

This spot has been a place of worship since ancient times. The two rocks are said to represent the male and female principles. People come here for purification, bathing in or drinking from a nearby waterfall before visiting the famous nearby shrine at Ise.

This area of Japan is especially sacred to the Shinto religion. About 2,000 years ago the daughter of Emperor Suinin spent twenty years wandering around Japan searching for a suitable place to build a shrine to the Sun Goddess Amaterasu. Arriving here, she heard, "This is a secluded and pleasant land. In this land I wish to dwell." The grand shrine of Ise has actually become a complex of 125 separate shrines. The current High Priestess in charge is Emperor Emeritus Akihito's daughter Sayako Kuroda.

Some traditions connect Amaterasu also to snakes and to dragons: "I have heard that the Sun Goddess of Ise … conceals her true being in the august image of Vairocana, and that she has appeared in the world in the guise of a dragon god of the blue ocean."[9]

Ise Rocks Stormy. Photo: Ron Balamuth

§

Listening to Stone

Two large stones were brought
To stand near the building where we live and work.
Standing stones – rooted, erect.

It is clear that they listen and I do not.
Standing near one, touching its surface
Something begins to change
Inside.
As if I become aware of a hush
Not really a sound but a hush
Not only in the stone
Not only in me
But everywhere.
A hush in the movement of the unfolding world.
I feel a hand on my shoulder
A gesture of recognition and support.
Together we stand – rooted, erect
And listening.

"Hear stone growing in a cliff"[10]

§§§

24. A Sacred Rune

An unknown object is dropped
Into the pool of my awareness.
Circles of a specific wavelength
Move out beyond my ken.
There is a light behind the forehead
That tells me I do not have the right
Not to speak.
I inhabit an organism
The gift of angels from the great beyond.
It is connected up and down and sideways
To many things.
How I use it evokes either creation or dissolution.
The sunlight of a brilliant winter morning
Allows this organism of mine to settle
Now.
Settle out of time
Into silence.
Not all silences are the same.
This one hums a soundless sound.
An atmosphere comes in
Billowing gently
Warm and
Supportive.
Wordlessly I am told,
"Do not worry.
Hold to the ascent.
Sense all the others who move with you now.
All will be well.
Heaven and Earth are one."

§§§

25. Alignment and Orientation

Malta is a tiny, now independent, country of two main islands plus a few small uninhabited ones sitting in just about the middle of the Mediterranean Sea: 58 miles (93 km) south of Sicily and 180 miles (288 km) north of Africa. On these two islands there are altogether thirteen officially recognized sites of megalithic temples plus a number of unofficial ones. Recalibrated radiocarbon dating has identified that these temples were constructed over a very long stretch of time from 5,000 BCE to 700 BCE. Until the recent excavation of Göbekli Tepe in Anatolian Turkey, where temple elements were carefully dated to 10,000 BCE, the temples on Malta used to be known as the oldest megalithic temples in the world.

"Megalithic" means "big stone." So we're talking about big stone temples. Using a fancy word makes it sound like we know what we're talking about. But the stones are only the skeletal remains of something that was once alive. Their original configurations were created from the force of their builders' hearts and minds. Now the remnants lie scattered. It is interesting that Göbekli Tepe was not abandoned, it was deliberately buried. Why was it hidden? Was it so that it could be discovered intact some 12,000 years later?

Given that we now understand something of the non-linear nature of time, let us speak with an architect who was involved in the creation of the temple complex located in the town of Tarxien, Malta. (Tarxien is pronounced "tar shin" with stress on the first syllable.)

In the Wikipedia article entitled "Tarxien Temples," there

is an image captioned “Altar in the southwestern Tarxien Temple” that powerfully pulls you in.

§

Trylus: I am an ignorant stranger here. Please tell me, “Why was this structure built?”

Architect: *What a bizarre question! Although you are looking a little pale and ghostly, you are standing with me here in one of the most sacred locations on this planet. Can you not feel that? Are you not penetrated through and through by the strength of its vibration, by its energetic force?*

Trylus: Erh… I feel something but it’s not very clear.

Architect: *That’s because you are scattered. Come, pull yourself together, man. Sharpen your awareness. Stop letting it wander.*

Trylus: OK.

Architect: *No, no. Not the awareness in your mind! The awareness in your body and feelings. There. That’s better, yes.*

Trylus: I am beginning to feel now that there is a connection between my feeling the lines of force and the spiral patterns on what the archeologists are calling an “altar” stone.

Architect: *Ah, yes. I see. Your time period is coming into focus for me now. Goodness, goodness – what disarray. What we built with such precision and care has been allowed to tumble down. And parts have been put back together in weird and senseless configurations. There is no understanding. The people living here now are like animals – only concerned about their stomachs and their safety. They are focused even less than you are now managing to do and their minds run riot, speculating what these structures are for instead of focusing on the energetic flow so they could see what they are for.*

Trylus: I begin to feel that some parts function as accumulators.

Architect: *Bravo! Of course, that is basic. And simple. But more important and more complex are the functions of receiving and transmitting. Alignment and orientation are critical.*

Trylus: Is the stone with spirals really an altar stone?

Architect: *The word "altar" is peculiar because I have the impression that you and your kind don't really understand what the word actually means.*

Trylus: Tell me more.

Architect: *An altar is designed to bring about an equilibrium and the spirals are a way of not only representing that action but also of engendering it. Once you become incarnated on this planet, it is essential to maintain a sensible balance between what is above you and what is below you.*

Trylus: Can you say what you mean by above and below.

Architect: *Well, if you insist... What is above is that which is of a higher vibration or a higher dimension of existence, finer, more powerful. And what is below you is that which you are deliberately entering into in order to fulfill your role of bringing the higher into the lower in order to actualize a new middle ground on which to stand, incarnated.*

Trylus: So then this is what these buildings are for – to help fulfill this role. Am I right?

Architect: *To state the obvious, yes!*

Trylus: And the alignment and orientation then also relate to what is above and what is below.

Architect: *Most certainly.*

Trylus: How did your civilization acquire this knowledge?

Architect: *Very simple. It was passed on to us by those who knew more than we did about the structure of the unfolding universe.*

Trylus: Is that a possibility for our civilization as well?

Architect: *Perhaps. If ever your scientists could stop using their minds to attempt to spin gold out of straw.*

Trylus: And how could such a change come about?

Architect: *Through alignment: Alignment with the forces that have the power to engender positive change such as those found here where we stand and which even the remnants of our stone structures still partially support.*

Trylus: My heart overflows with gratitude for your help.

Architect: *Don't let it overflow much; keep it for your own path. You will need it brother. The way ahead is long.*

Trylus: You do feel like a brother to me now.

Architect: *The altar has jogged your memory. Let us quietly rejoice.*

§§§

26. A Promise from On High

Saint Catherine's Monastery

The brown of the rocky Sinai desert is unremitting and stark. After traveling through this landscape for hours, an approach to the monastery is signaled by the piercing green of tall cypress in and around the high ochre walls of the compound.

Coming from Jerusalem, in the 1970s, I traveled first to the Israeli resort and shipping port of Eilat, located on the Red Sea at the northern tip of the Gulf of Aqaba. This voyage was before the Sinai Peninsula, which Israel had captured in the Six Day War of June 1967, was returned to Egypt in

1982. Israel however retained access to Eilat, and thereby to the Red Sea and beyond, by keeping a triangular wedge of land squeezed between Jordan on the east and the Sinai on the west. Security was strict during my trip and included a full body pat down and a hands-on search through my afro haircut.

Saint Catherine's was built between 548 and 565 CE and is one of the oldest continuously operational Christian monasteries. It rests at the base of Mount Sinai where Moses received the tablets of the Ten Commandments. The mountain is sacred to all three Abrahamic religions: Judaism, Christianity, and Islam.

The Prophet Muhammad (570-632 CE) is said to have visited and to have enjoyed his stay among the monks. Perhaps as a result of this visit, Muhammad wrote a letter granting special protection and privileges for Christians living under Muslim rule. Copies of the letter are displayed prominently in the monastery's library. The original document is part of the archival collection at the Topkapi Palace in Istanbul.

Certain scholars question the authenticity of this letter not realizing that the authenticity of the sentiments it contains far outweigh their scholarly deliberations.

During the reign of the 6th Fatimid Caliph Al-Hakim bi-Amr Allah (996 to 1021 CE), a Crusader church within the monastery's fortified walls was converted to a mosque with its minaret opposite the monastery's bell tower. From its dedication to the present day, the mosque has been a sanctuary for prayer for the Bedouin and Arab neighbors who live and work near or in the monastery.

§

The Prophet Muhammad's Visit

Trylus: Tell me about this visit.

Abbot: *He shone with great light, a dazzling white light. As he approached the burning bush, it too began to quiver and shine.*

Trylus: Did he come alone?

Abbot: *No, not alone, but with a very few trusted companions.*

Trylus: Why did he visit?

Abbot: *It was a pilgrimage of sorts and the journey was not easy. But it was to fulfill a wish to be in the presence of the mountain beside our monastery that bears Moses's name, Jabal Musa* [Mount Sinai in English]. *Knowing what Moses had to endure and his perseverance, he wanted to visit and feel for himself the nature and qualities of the place.*

Trylus: What did he say about it?

Abbot: *He said little or nothing about his experience, but it was clear that his heart was full of gratitude. It poured forth from his eyes.*

Trylus: Were there discussions at mealtime?

Abbot: *The meals were silent. Each one of us immersed in individual contemplation. But afterwards, in small gatherings, there was some exchange.*

Trylus: What interested him?

Abbot: *He was interested that formerly, and not that long before his visit, our monastery was originally dedicated to the mother of Jesus. I was surprised to hear him say that he preferred that designation.*

Trylus: Did he give a reason for that preference?

Abbot: *He said that Mariam* [as the Holy Mother is called in Arabic] *is worthy of veneration and that contemplating her elevated level of attainment is advisable for any truly devout person, man or woman. He spoke of her with the greatest respect.*

Trylus: What else can be said about this visit?

Abbot: *He said that the visit was like a seal or a signet.*

Trylus: In what way?

Abbot: *He said that our monastery was and would be like a promise of the good to come – that in some far distant time, the strife that is so prevalent in the human world will end. Men and women will come to live in peace and harmony, just as the brethren here manage to do. He ended by saying, "Your having welcomed me here is ample proof of that promise, a promise which comes from On High."*

§ § §

27. Redeeming the Sacred
The Oracle of Delphi

The oracle of Delphi was located on the slopes of Mount Parnassus, about 100 miles (160 km) north-west of Athens, Greece. The presence of an oracle at this site spans nearly 2,000 years, stretching back perhaps as far as 1400 BCE or even earlier and continuing until the fourth century CE.

Initially, the oracle was under the tutelage of the Earth goddess, Gaia. But around 800 BCE, the Greek god Apollo brutally displaced Gaia by killing her serpent named Python who was protecting her and also protecting the omphalos or navel of the world. The sky god Zeus located this navel by sending two eagles off from either of the Earth's extremities. Their paths crossed at Delphi thus marking the location. A carved marble representation of the omphalos was found by archeologists at Delphi. Omphalos stones were believed to allow direct communication with the gods.

In another version of the story, Apollo expelled the twin guardian serpents of Gaia, placing them entwined on a staff called "caduceus." This staff, sometimes surmounted by wings, is carried in the left hand of the speedy messenger god Hermes who was known to the Romans as Mercury. Three thousand years earlier than Apollo, a staff with two entwined serpents was the symbol of the Sumerian god Ningishzida, Lord of the Good Tree.

The voice of the oracle at Delphi was always that of a woman, although male priests at the site may have acted as interpreters of what she spoke. She would sit on a tripod over cracks in the earth from which vapors arose that promoted her connection to the special state required for her to converse with the gods. This was thought to have been a fanciful story until recently when it was discovered that this zone, which is prone to tectonic plate movement, has bitumen (petroleum) deposits that could release ethylene, a gas capable of producing changes in states of consciousness. Ethylene is described as having a "sweet and musky" smell, which matches contemporary descriptions of the vapors rising up around the tripod.

The duty priestess was called Pythia (Πυθία). She also used a shallow dish of water to see images from the invisible world – a technique that is called "skrying."

Carved above the doorway to her temple, was the maxim, "Know thyself" (γνῶθι σεαυτόν, *gnōthi seautón*).

Two other principal maxims were "Nothing in excess" (μηδὲν ἄγαν, *mēdén ágan*) and "Make a pledge and mischief is at hand" (Ἐγγύα πάρα δ'ἄτη, *engýa pára d'atē*). This third maxim indicates that "Going with the flow" is a concept that antedates the 1960 period of the Western world. The Greek goddess Atē mentioned in this maxim is the goddess of mischief, delusion, ruin, and folly.

The story that comes down to us is always the one trumpeted by the conqueror. What is the story that Gaia needs us to hear? Her guardian the serpent has been killed, usurped or defamed. Her priestess repurposed. Let us ask.

§

Gaia's Words of Wisdom

Trylus: Some humans now begin to awaken to your needs. What do you advise?

Gaia: *Humans have a potential to shine, although most are dim.*

Trylus: Can you say more?

Gaia: *Bring your light to the transition that is now underway – the movement toward an awareness that the natural world is sacred and ought to be treated as such. Such an awareness is rare* *among you.*

Trylus: Most have no awareness of what the word "sacred" even means.

Gaia: *Yes. That is evident. But it can be learned from those who know.*

Trylus: Do you mean that some humans do know?

Gaia: *A few, yes. But, also humans can, through their capacity to feel, experience the sacred through what they choose to be open to. Ask, and a spirit guide or an angel may respond. In this way, one can be instructed without the severe limitations of human language.*

Trylus: The serpent has been maligned since the time when Delphi changed hands. What attitude is helpful in this regard?

Gaia: (smiling) *Well, one could remember that Jesus said to his apostles, "Behold, I send you forth as sheep in the midst of wolves: be ye therefore wise as serpents, and harmless as doves" [Matthew 10:16, KJV]. Such wisdom is very much lacking and humans should realize that the serpent embodies it. This tradition is ancient and widespread. It is already beginning to return.*

Trylus: What went wrong in the Garden of Eden?

Gaia: *An initiation to the sacred failed. It can now be redeemed.*

Trylus: Is there reason to be hopeful?

Gaia: *Hope, if conscious, is strength. Be conscious. Be strong.*

Trylus: I bow to your presence.

Gaia: *And I to yours.*

§ § §

28. The Three Sisters

"The Three Sisters" is the modern name of three small islands in the Saint Lawrence River opposite Brockville, Ontario to the north and Morristown, New York to the south. In aboriginal lore, these three islands announce the beginning of the Thousand Islands chain of idyllic islands that lie dotted through the massive Saint Lawrence River, upstream toward Lake Ontario. These three particular islands were considered sacred by the first nations people who lived in the area. They were harbingers, but also protective spirits to be consulted as people's needs might dictate.

I feel saddened by how those original native people must feel at these islands' current condition. No one cares for them in any way. What little grows there now is sparse and scrawny.

The most northerly of the three sisters is defaced with an ugly concrete structure, part of a bridge that was never completed.

For about 15 years now, I have fairly regularly gone to sit by the Saint Lawrence River and pay my respects to these islands. I'm not sure I knew that's what I was doing, but it did feel that way. For some reason, I have always felt a connection and never thought much about it until now. However, engaged as I am in this "writing project," I have become aware that a channel of communication has been present for some time. So I feel emboldened to ask:

Trylus: Is it true that I hear you crying, "Pray for us! Pray for us!"?

The Three Sisters: *Of course. Why would you doubt what you hear? Be the warrior you truly are.*

Trylus: I live in a time of great darkness and destruction. The land is laid waste as you know. But I sense there is hope in the light on the moving blue of the river. I feel a new time coming.

The Three Sisters: *We* know *that a new time is coming and we know that we may or may not survive. Tankers pass us every day taking the planet's lifeblood to be burned. And the Earth has told us, "Not long now. A new time is coming. Listen to my promise: No matter what happens, you will have your place even if it might be on a mountain top or in the depths of the sea. My heart will always remember your role and the service you have performed."*

Trylus: Can I help?

The Three Sisters: *You* have *helped. Almost the only one who has helped – for centuries. We feel you touch us with your mind and heart. And it helps. We have greeted you in return, and recently you have begun to notice.*

Trylus: Thank you. I will notice more clearly now. You are my sisters.

The Three Sisters: *And you our brother true. May the Great Spirit protect you and be with you. Always.*

The Three Sisters, Aerial View
©Ian Coristine 1000IslandsPhotoArt.com

§§§

29. A 2020 Cry

Swathed in flowing multi-colored robes
And trailing glory does he come
Across the fields and plains of desolation
and despair.

"Look! Look! On high" rings out his cry
As trumpeting angels descend

And clouds are parted for the brilliant disc
to shine.

Scurrying humans stumble to and fro,
confused and unaware
That above their busy heads
An era ends/begins.
Oh Herald of the coming good
Bestow upon us now
Your Grace, your Love
And may we blessèd be,
Serving singly and as one
The sweetness of Heaven's reign.

§§§

30. Grasp the Azure

It is said we must grasp the azure[11]
But not with the hands
Or with the head.
First it must be seen –
For rarely does it appear –
Only at the most unexpected moments
And at the most unlikely of places –
Abandoned places, watery places, forgotten places
Where one thing turns into another.
And once seen
What is it that can reach out?

What inner faculty can touch?
I see a hand inadvertently reach out
And in the azure it dissolves.
I am dumb.
And I am dumbfounded.
As I stand before it,
Upright and aligned,
The azure begins to stir.
Connections begin to form.
Voices of the ancients murmur in the dark
As I remember who I am.
But it is partial
And unclear.
The azure billows now.
Its movement draws me in.
Dead things fall away.

I know nothing.
I am nothing.
I hear,
"Drink the laughter of the sun
And thrive."

Azure Life

§§§

Contents

Notes

1 To honor my father, with whom I had a tenuous relationship, I use his middle name "Trylus" (Robert Trylus Cain) as my company name. I do this to stress that in dialogues such as this one both parts of the dialogue are "received material" and are not my personal voice. [Ch 3: The Next Step; Dialogue; paragraph 1]

2 The petroglyph images may be viewed in: Joan M. Vastokas and Romas K. Vastokas, *Sacred Art of the Algonkians: A Study of the Peterborough Petroglyphs*, Peterborough, Ontario, Mansard Press, 1973. Image 1: p. 56; image 2: p. 121; image 3: p. 66. Also, an Internet search will easily turn up the first two; the third has been less often reproduced. The book is out-of-print and rare; try looking for it in a library or on inter-library loan. [Ch 6: paragraph 4]

3 For a more complete version of Ingo's report see: Russell Targ, *The Reality of ESP: A Physicist's Proof of Psychic Abilities*, Quest Books, 2012, pp. 30-32. [Ch 8: paragraph 2]

4 This poem was inspired by watching a videoclip about a blind falconer, Norbek, who won, or rather his falcon Oymuk won, the gold medal in the 2018 World Nomad Games.
https://www.youtube.com/watch?v=QyeBxcvUJIU
The story is at 5:31 to 6:40 minutes within the video link above. [Ch 8: end of poem "Sensible"]

5 An Aeolian harp or wind harp is a stringed instrument played by the wind. It is named after the Greek god of wind, Aeolus. [Ch 9: See: "Aeolian harp" in the middle of the dialogue]

6 *The Yongle Palace Murals*, 1st ed., Beijing, Foreign Languages Press, 1985, p. 48. Modern pinyin spelling of his name: Cangjie. [Ch 14: paragraph 2 of the dialogue]

7 These four directives are documented in: *Los Templos del Cielo y de la Oscuridad: Oráculos y Liturgia. Libro explicativo del llamado Códice Borgia.* In the native language the four are: Ka Nishpopoyotl, Ka Nitlayowalli, Ka Shomolli, Ka Nikaltechtli. [Ch 16: line 7]

8 *The Essential Haiku: Versions of Bashō, Buson, and Issa*, edited and with verse translation by Robert Hass, The Ecco Press, 1994, p. 233. [Ch 20: dialogue paragraph 2]

9 Bernard Fauré, *Protectors and Predators: Gods of Medieval Japan*, vol. 2, University of Hawaii Press. [Ch 23: line before second image]

10 Who will prefer the jingle of jade pendants if he once has heard stone growing in a cliff?" *The Way of Life According to Lao Tzu*, translated by Witter Bynner, Penguin, 1995. [Ch 23: Photo caption at the end of the poem "Listening to Stone"]

11 Confucius, *Ta Hsüeh (The Great Learning)*, verse 2: "Know the point of rest and then have an orderly mode of procedure; having this orderly procedure one can 'grasp the azure,' that is, take hold of a clear concept." Ezra Pound's translation. New Directions, 1969, p. 29. [Ch 30: Poem line 1]

§§§

Acknowledgements

First and foremost an ocean of gratitude is due to my highly competent editor/friend Müge Galin who caught many a slip of the tongue and eye and inspired a number of critical re-writes and emendations.

A special place is reserved in my heart for Richard Wilde who pioneered initial efforts to get this material out into the world.

David Appelbaum's never faltering encouragement was also key… as was his publishing from Codhill Press my 2019 book of poems *In the Region of the Heart*.

Conti Canseco Meehan brought ongoing refinements in heart-felt words.

And then there are the many other friends who frequently reassured me that all is flowing as it should: Kate Breithaupt, formerly a producer with CBC Canada, Patty de Llosa, author of *Taming the Inner Tyrant* and other titles, Rosanne Weston, Sophia Cowing, and M'Lou Caring in New York, Richard Whittaker, Mary Stein, Nancy Veith, and Mimi Fain in San Francisco and Paulina Hernandez in Mexico City.

My spirit realm guides of course already know the place in my heart reserved to honor their unfailing support.

§§§

Jack at Burnt Island, Michigan,
Labor Day Weekend 2023
Photo: Benjamin Rae

About the Author

Jack Cain

Attended Snowball Public School in Ontario, Canada: a one-room, red brick building with a pot-bellied wood stove for heat in the winter. Did university. Learned French. Studied Chinese. Wrote haiku for a while. Enjoyed a stimulating career in library automation, punctuated with repeated visits to clients in Japan, Taiwan, and Korea. For Asian libraries, designed and implemented a Unicode system before Unicode computer encoding existed. Dabbled in linguistics. Translated 20 books from French to English. Helped computerize the Inuit language, Inuktitut.

At retirement age, trained in and began using altered states of consciousness (still misnamed "hypnosis"), and an energy modality called Reconnective Healing™ to help seekers with their journey through terrestrial life. (www.trylus.com)

Fell in love with Mexico. Learned some Spanish.

Listening skills in perceiving and deciphering spirit voices have gradually improved. Thus dialogues now flow

The wandering scribe bends to his appointed task.

www.ingramcontent.com/pod-product-compliance
Lightning Source LLC
LaVergne TN
LVHW052354100826
845147LV00013B/836
* 9 7 8 1 9 6 0 0 9 0 5 0 8 *